Lost in translation

A complete guide to Chair/Chief Executive partnerships

Written by Tesse Akpeki

Edited by Marta Maretich

NCVO produces a wide range of accessible books and reports for organisations working in the voluntary and community sector. Subjects covered include:

- Trustee and governance
- Employment and diversity
- Finance and sustainable funding
- Managing, marketing and communications
- Voluntary sector research and policy
- Performance improvement

For more information about the complete range of NCVO titles, go to www.ncvo-vol.org.uk/publications or phone NCVO's HelpDesk free on 0800 2 798 798.

Members of NCVO receive a 30% discount on all titles, and membership is free for organisations with an income of less than £10,000 per year. To find out more, go to www.ncvo-vol.org.uk/membership or ring our Membership team on 020 7520 2414.

Published by NCVO
Regent's Wharf All Saints Street London N1 9RL

Published July 2006

© NCVO 2006
Registered Charity Number: 225922

Written by Tesse Akpeki
Edited by Marta Maretich
Design by Philip Pestell, NCVO
Printed by Latimer Trend and Company Ltd

British Library Cataloguing in Public Data
A catalogue record for this book is available from the British Library

ISBN: 0 7199 1670 4

Every effort has been made to ensure the accuracy of the information contained within this publication. However, NCVO cannot be held responsible for any action an individual or organisation takes, or fails to take, as a result of this information.

Table of contents

	Page
Foreword by Su Sayer, OBE, Chief Executive of United Response	i
Introduction: The Chief Executive/Chair partnership in context	1
Part 1: Understanding roles and responsibilities	5
Role of the Chair	5
Model documents for the role of Chair	11
Role of the Chief Executive	14
Model documents for the role of Chief Executive	19
Part 2: Relationship profiles	23
Portrait of a partnership	23
Patterns in different organisations	24
When the partners aren't equal	26
Part 3: Building healthy partnerships	27
Establishing core policies	27
Selecting a Chair who can partner the Chief Executive	28
Establishing the partnership	29
Improving communication	32
Making the most of shared responsibilities	36
Part 4: Dealing with conflict	43
Avoiding conflict	43
Handling conflict when it arises	44
Resources	47
Organisations	47
Publications	48
Model documents for the role of Chair (for photocopy purposes)	49
Model documents for the role of Chief Executive (for photocopy purposes)	51

Foreword

As a Chief Executive with over 30 years' experience, I am a firm believer in the importance of a good working relationship with your Chair. Indeed, it is partly as a result of the partnership I had with my first Chair, that I am where I am today.

I set up United Response (UR), a national charity which supports people with learning disabilities or mental health needs, in 1973, together with my first Chair, Ernest Kleinwort. We shared a vision – to support people with learning disabilities to live in the community, and to enjoy the rights and choices that most people take for granted. This was at a time when people with learning disabilities were shut away in long stay hospitals and institutions – the idea of supporting people in ordinary houses in the community was unheard of. Yet, thanks to the positive working relationship I had with my Chair, and our shared passion and commitment to really make a difference, we were able to set up our very first house for people with learning disabilities in West Sussex.

Today, UR is a top 100 charity, employing over 2000 staff and with a turnover for 06/07 predicted to hit the £48 million mark. We support 1500 people with learning disabilities or mental health needs across the country to lives they choose. It is – of course – a very different organisation from the one we set up thirty years ago. But one constant through all that time, growth and change has been the vital importance of working in partnership with my Chair.

In my experience, the connection between the Chief Executive and Chair is an important part of what makes voluntary and community sector organisations strong, resilient and effective.

My Chairs have been talented, dedicated individuals who shared my passion for our mission, gave me the benefit of their expertise and worked with me to develop our organisation and ensure that we had a strong and skilled Board.

Our dialogue is the point of contact between the how and the why of the organisation. And, when my Board and Chair challenge me and my senior team (and they do often) it forces us to engage with governance in a way which enriches our work and makes us all more responsible executives. The effect of our work is synergy, a combination that is far stronger than the component parts.

In the absence of an effective Chair/Chief Executive partnership, this meeting of minds proves difficult if not impossible. Knowing that their partnership is a cornerstone of organisational success, many Chief Executives and Chairs are actively engaged in seeking better ways to work together. Lost in translation offers a needed resource for Chief Executives, Chairs and for trustee boards as they begin the process of building a Chief Executive/Chair relationship that really serves the organisation.

Su Sayer, OBE
Chief Executive of United Response

Sponsor's foreword

The Principle Partnership, a division of TPP Newman

The Principle Partnership is delighted to sponsor NCVO's *Lost in Translation: a survival guide for Chairs and CEOs*. Having specialised in recruiting to the charity and not-for-profit sector for over 10 years, our experience and knowledge of these areas is extensive. By working with voluntary and community organisations to assist them in recruiting Executive positions, our experience tells us that an effective and healthy Chair/CEO relationship is critical to the success of the organisation in meeting the needs of beneficiaries now, and in responding to their future needs.

We are particularly pleased to support a guide that offers readers practical support and help that will enable them to refresh their working relationship and address the issues that can often hinder this crucial partnership.

Lost in Translation also includes a list of further resources to point Chairs and CEOs in the direction of further advice and help if it is needed.

The Principle Partnership is very pleased to have the opportunity to support a tool that will help Chairs and CEOs do what they do well better, and address common relationship pitfalls in a pragmatic and creative way.

The Principle Partnership
www.tpp.co.uk
020 7198 6000

The Principle Partnership
specialist recruitment consultants

Introduction: The Chief Executive/Chair partnership in context

In recent years, much has been written and said about the importance of the personal relationship between the Chair and the Chief Executive in voluntary and community sector organisations. The quality of the one-to-one rapport between these leaders is frequently credited for organisational success – or blamed for a host of problems. The focus is often on personalities or personal working styles and the tendency is to talk of the Chief Executive/Chair partnership as a marriage.

There is no doubt that the quality of the working relationship between Chief Executive and Chair is very important to voluntary and community sector organisations and that personality plays a role in shaping it. Yet to see this relationship in purely personal terms is to overlook its real significance. In fact, the Chief Executive/Chair relationship is a key component of an effective governance system. When it works the way it should, it provides a vital interface between the executive and the governing body, assuring accountability and facilitating strategic engagement. When it fails, the quality of governance suffers.

Beyond interpersonal relationships

For this reason, the issues that arise between Chief Executives and Chairs cannot be addressed solely on the level of interpersonal dynamics. Their relations are supported – or thwarted – by their context. Organisations need to learn to look beyond personalities and see that Chief Executive/Chair relations are shaped as much by structural factors as they are by individual behaviour. This approach empowers boards, Chairs and Chief Executives alike to take practical steps to improve the quality of the Chief Executive/Chair relationship, turning it into an effective partnership with the power to serve the organisation.

Lost in translation places the Chief Executive/Chair relationship in a governance context, showing how good policy, well-planned systems and a framework of support can transform this relationship. Based on NCVO's hands-on experience advising numerous organisations, its approach combines practical advice with the latest guidance from top governance experts and authorities such as ACEVO, CEDR and the Governance Hub. For the first time, *Lost in translation* offers a practical guide for boards and managers looking for ways to foster good personal relations, remove obstacles to partnership and encourage strong leadership from Chief Executives and Chairs.

Loaded with useful tips, practical techniques and helpful information *Lost in translation* speaks directly to Chief Executives, Chairs, trustees and trainers, bringing them the information they need to start work on improving Chief Executive/Chair effectiveness today. It takes readers step-by-step through the many structural factors influencing partnership from recruitment and selection processes to communication practice. It examines the role of the board in establishing a climate that supports organisational leaders, bringing clarity to their individual and joint work. And it shows how interventions, such as governance development, skill training, facilitation and mediation can help make more of the Chief Executive/Chair working relationship.

Achieving role clarity

Role clarity is one key to establishing an effective Chief Executive/Chair partnership and *Part 1: Understanding roles and responsibilities*, is dedicated to this important question. It examines the multiple role of the Chair as trustee, organisational leader, board/staff liaison and strategic partner to the Chief Executive, giving detailed guidance on how Chairs can make the most of each of these vital functions. It also outlines the role of the Chief Executive and offers insights into how the executive can optimise his/her work with the board and get needed support from the Chair. Model job descriptions and person specifications are included to act as a starting point for board discussion as they undertake the essential process of defining Chief Executive and Chair roles in their organisation.

It can be difficult to envision an effective Chair/Chief Executive partnership, especially if you've never experienced one. *Part 2: Relationship profiles*, gives an overview of how a healthy Chief Executive/Chair partnership contributes to effective governance practice, acting as an invaluable conduit for communication and fostering strategic cooperation between the governing body and the executive. A selection of shorter profiles shows how the Chief Executive/Chair partnership may differ in relationships of different sizes, facing different circumstances.

Positive steps

Part 3: Building healthy partnerships offers a guide to the actions organisations and individual Chief Executives and Chairs can take to make partnership work. First, it outlines important board policies that form the basis for joint work: vision, mission and values. Then it provides guidance for laying the groundwork of a partnership by choosing the right individuals through good selection and recruitment processes.

The early days of any partnership are critical to its success. *Building healthy partnerships* offers practical advice on ways to get partnership off on the right foot by creating a Chief Executive/Chair working agreement. Communication is also important, and this guide provides a detailed framework for improving the whole communication environment for your organisation, starting with broad, organisation-wide policies and working toward policies designed specifically to make communication between Chief Executive and Chair all it should be.

Dealing with conflict

Context plays a large part in shaping Chief Executive/Chair partnerships, yet there is no doubt that Chief Executives and Chairs need a decent relationship to work well together. *Lost in translation* offers many valuable tips and techniques to help individuals build a good personal rapport. *Part 4: Dealing with conflict* goes a step farther, offering expert advice on how to avoid clashes and what to do when partnerships turn sour. It describes the practical techniques–including facilitated discussion and mediation–that can help Chief Executives and Chairs turn a troubled relationship around.

Lost in translation offers more than an overview of the Chief Executive/Chair partnership in context. It contains exercises, pointers, useful facts and techniques drawn from our extensive hands-on experience with Chief Executives and Chairs. Finally, a useful resource section points the way to agencies, websites and publications that offer even more support for Chief Executive/Chair partnerships.

7 things Chief Executives and Chairs need for successful partnership

Chief Executives and Chairs don't operate in a vacuum. For the partnership to succeed they need a framework of basic support from the organisation.

1 Clearly defined roles on both sides

Many problems between Chief Executives and Chairs grow out of a simple confusion about roles. Job descriptions, person specifications and good training for both parties help lay the groundwork for an effective partnership.

2 A shared vision

Without a shared sense of purpose Chief Executives and Chairs may end up working toward different goals. A common vision helps them avoid conflict and join forces for greater effectiveness.

3 Basic behaviour guidelines

Good will is not always enough to maintain the level of cooperation Chief Executives and Chairs need to work together. Detailed codes of conduct for the Chair and the Chief Executive help individuals behave in ways that support partnership working.

4 A policy framework

The trustee board sets the stage for a successful partnership by providing a sound framework of written organisational policy for both parties to work with. By setting clear guidelines, the board minimises the problems caused by confusion, role ambiguity or personal disagreements.

5 Good communication systems

Communication is key to the Chief Executive/Chair partnership. By establishing good communication policies and practices, organisations support the Chief Executive/Chair relationship and help them work at the top of their game.

6 Development opportunities

Development can bring new effectiveness to the Chief Executive/Chair partnership. Chief Executive and Chair can also collaborate on devising development for the board, thus improving governance overall.

7 A way to get help

Both Chief Executive and Chair should be able to count on individual support and development, built into the structure of their jobs. Both should have a clear procedure for dealing with complaints and grievances. Finally they should be able to get support for their partnership through services like facilitation and mediation.

Part 1

Understanding roles and responsibilities

In NCVO's recent work with Chief Executives and Chairs in the Barclay's Leadership Programme, one factor stands out as a crucial element in an effective partnership: a clear, correct understanding of roles and responsibilities on both sides. This section provides detailed guidelines about how organisations can improve partnership by defining the roles of Chief Executive and Chair.

Role of the Chair

A Chair (short for Chairman, Chairwoman or Chairperson) is a trustee who is appointed by his or her fellow trustees to lead the board in its governance activities. He or she has a dual role as team member, having the same responsibilities as any trustee, and team leader, with the extra duties and responsibilities of leadership.

Mainly, the Chair serves the board by doing or overseeing much of the practical work that enables the group to carry out governance responsibilities in a systematic and accountable way. Logically, Chair duties will vary somewhat from organisation to organisation, but the core role remains the same in all organisations, defined by the standards of good governance practice set out in *Good Governance: a code for the voluntary and community sector*, available from NCVO and the Governance Hub (see Resources).

All organisations must create a written role description for the Chair. This key document, along with an accompanying person specification, helps strengthen the role in a number of ways. Essential to the processes of Chair recruitment and induction, a clear role description and person specification are also invaluable to Chairs as they work alongside their opposite number, the Chief Executive. Reviewed regularly by the board and kept up to date they support both the work of the individual Chair and governance practice overall. For a complete Chair job description and person specification, turn to the model documents at the end of this section.

For an introduction to the Chair's role see *The Chair's first 100 days* by Tesse Akpeki. For an in-depth guide to the roles and responsibilities of the Chair, see Dorothy Dalton's comprehensive *Good governance: the Chair's role*, available from NCVO.

12 core Chair responsibilities

1 ensuring governance activity complies with regulations and good practice

2 planning the annual schedule of board meetings

3 devising meeting agendas, leading meetings and facilitating discussion

4 making sure board decisions are communicated to the Chief Executive for implementation

5 taking appropriate action on behalf of the board between meetings, as authorised

6 managing and overseeing the work of committees

7 overseeing the board's management of the Chief Executive

8 working with the Chief Executive to foster board strategic engagement

9 supporting and developing the Chief Executive

10 leading board development activity including regular self-assessment

11 recruiting trustees and preparing Chair succession

12 representing the organisation at functions and meetings, acting as spokesperson when appropriate

A word about delegation

A glance at the list of Chair responsibilities shows that the role can be demanding. Experienced Chairs agree that delegation is the key to avoiding burnout. Board officers, especially the Vice Chair, Honorary Treasurer, committees and committee leaders, even members of staff and volunteers can all be enlisted to help the Chair with regular duties. Oversight is the key: the Chair needs to manage delegation, set goals for those doing the work, and then monitor that the work is done properly. A written brief for committees, and a role description for officers helps Chairs delegate securely.

Though many tasks can be safely delegated, the most strategically important work should always be done by the Chair him- or herself. For this reason, most of the work the Chair carries out in partnership with the Chief Executive should not be delegated to others. The exception is during Chief Executive appraisal when the Chair lacks the necessary background or skills to evaluate Chief Executive performance properly. In this case, the Chair can select another trustee or officer to carry out the appraisal on his or her behalf or the organisation can introduce outside consultants to help with the evaluation, provided the Chair oversees the process and answers for the result.

The Chair and the Chief Executive

The Chair, as leader of the board, has a special, multi-faceted relationship with the Chief Executive.

- First, the Chair leads the board as it carries out basic management duties toward its top executive by coordinating various oversight duties such as Chief Executive appraisal.

- Second, the Chair acts as a primary point of contact between the executive and the governing body, working to maintain accountability, good relations and a constant flow of information between these two parts of the organisation.

- Third, the Chair shares with the Chief Executive a joint leadership role. Working together they inspire and motivate the organisation.

- Finally, the Chair acts as strategic partner to the Chief Executive, guiding the board as it develops strategic ability and using governance practice to support strategic aims.

Facilitating the board's management of the Chief Executive

In voluntary and community sector organisations, the Chief Executive works directly for the trustee board. For the board, this managerial role brings with it a raft of responsibilities. It is up to the Chair to coordinate the work and lead the board as it fulfils its many obligations toward its top employee. These include:

Writing job descriptions and person specifications

These documents give the board strategic input on the role of the Chief Executive in their organisation. And they provide a basis for recruiting, hiring and assessment.

Determining remuneration

The trustee board can seek advice in this technical area, but the final decision of how to remunerate the Chief Executive is strategic and can only be taken by the governing board.

Hiring

The trustee board has the ultimate responsibility for recruiting, selecting and contracting a new Chief Executive.

Assessing performance

The board has the job of assessing or appraising Chief Executive performance. It needs to establish clear criteria for assessment and a regular schedule for carrying it out, offering feedback and taking any actions necessary in response to performance results.

Development

The board has a responsibility to cultivate its Chief Executive, offering support – both moral and material – and development opportunities to enhance skills and performance.

Discipline

When a problem arises with the Chief Executive, the board acts as a disciplinary body, determining the course of action to take in the best interests of the organisation.

Acting as a point of contact

As board leader and spokesperson for the group, the Chair acts as the main point of contact between the board and its Chief Executive. So important is this aspect of the Chair/Chief Executive relationship that organisations should provide written guidelines on how these two key figures will work together, how often they will meet, what behaviour they will use with one another and so on. Good communication is vital as are reliable systems to foster healthy interchange. Personality and individual skills also come into play, and specific development for both parties can improve the quality of their contact and enhance governance overall. For more detail on all these subjects, see *Part 3: Building healthy partnerships*.

The Chief Executive should also have an opportunity to work with other trustees and to speak directly to the board without the intermediary of the Chair. Similarly, the Chair may wish to communicate or work on projects with other staff members. This is fine, as long as the organisation offers specific guidelines on how these situations are to be handled. Some organisations avoid confusion by requiring both Chief Executive and Chair to let one another know ahead of time when they will be meeting with other staff or board members.

Joint Chief Executive/Chair leadership

When defining the role of the Chair with its many duties, it is easy for organisations to overlook what may ultimately be the most significant aspect of the role: as well as an effective board leader, the Chair should also be an organisational leader whose influence can be felt far from the boardroom. Credible, competent and knowledgeable, working with the endorsement of the governing body, and effective Chair has authority and should use it to motivate and inspire the organisation.

The Chair shares the role of overall organisational leader with the Chief Executive. For this reason, the quality of their partnership is fundamental to organisational success. Each partner carries the responsibility for different aspects of key activities such as strategy-making, reporting, financial accountability and risk management. But both share responsibility for forming an effective partnership and using their joint authority to provide vision, security and direction for the organisation.

Attitude

Attitude is everything when it comes to leadership. The Chair who understands his/her role, grasps the tenets of good governance and sees the Chief Executive as a partner, not an adversary, is already a long way toward becoming the kind of leader organisations need. A needlessly negative or aggressive Chair destroys the possibility of a real partnership with the Chief Executive. By demonstrating good will and developing a candid, challenging but supportive working relationship, the Chair can form an effective alliance between the board and the executive. The balance should be: close but critical when necessary, always cooperative but never cosy.

Preparation

To make the most of joint leadership, Chairs, even those new to the job, should aim for a sense of equality with the Chief Executive: an uninformed, dependent or passive Chair is little use to the organisation or the Chief Executive. (NCVO's recent surveys of Chief Executives show that executives long for Chairs who understand organisational issues and are willing to act as sources of support.) Chairs should take up all opportunities for induction, training, mentoring and coaching the organisation offers. If no such programmes exist, the Chair should use his or her position to establish them.

Active engagement

On the basis of adequate training, good governance systems and a healthy partnership with the Chief Executive, Chairs can share leadership in a number of ways:

- with the Chief Executive, taking a leading role in framing issues and bringing large-scale organisational change such as a governance overhaul;

- using his/her intimate knowledge of the board to help the Chief Executive present issues and convey information effectively;

- sharing the burden of bad news or hard times with the Chief Executive;

- working with trustees behind the scenes or taking on the role of spokesperson in public to promote initiatives and projects;

- developing his/her awareness of the present climate and potential future risks for the organisation;

- connecting to the larger voluntary and community sector (especially to networks of other Chairs) and encouraging the Chief Executive to do the same;

- seeking out new ideas and innovative techniques that can strengthen the organisation;

- working with the Chief Executive to find practical ways to improve the performance of the trustee board.

Part 1

> ## Keys to twin leadership
>
> ### Key elements
>
> - Good chairing skills (Chair)
> - No surprises (Chief Executive)
> - No public disagreements (Both)
>
> ### In public
>
> - Demonstrating mutual support (Both)
> - Avoiding the appearance of 'stitching things up' (Both)
> - Capacity to make informed decisions between meetings (Chair)
> - Ability to consult (Both)
>
> ### In private
>
> - Ability to challenge, criticise and give credit (Chair)
> - Ability to discuss, make diplomatic suggestions and give credit (Chief Executive)
>
> Winifred Tumin,
> *Workshop, Barclays Leadership Programme, October 2004*

Strategic partner to the Chief Executive

The Chair can maximise the effectiveness of the board and act as a support to the executive by strengthening the strategic engagement of the governing body.

Familiarising him/herself with the strategic plan

Every Chair needs to understand the overall strategic plan of his or her organisation. For some, this may mean studying an existing plan and asking questions of the Chief Executive and other officers to gain more insight into its meaning. Others may have the opportunity to work alongside the executive to formulate a plan. In any case, the Chair must use this plan as a basis for identifying agenda items for board meetings and planning board activities.

Creating strategic meeting agendas

Meeting agendas should be built around issues in the strategic plan. A well-prepared agenda that frames all topics strategically helps encourage the right level of decision making from the board. Chairs can enlist the Chief Executive to plan agendas that maximise the strategic value of board meeting agendas.

Guiding debate

The Chair has an important role in determining the quality of debate at board meetings. He or she influences discussions by managing group dynamics, guiding the direction of the conversation and bringing the issue to vote. To keep board debate productive, a Chair needs to be able to maintain a focus on the strategic core of the issue. Good meeting and facilitation skills, coupled with a strong strategic awareness, help him or her make meetings strategic occasions.

Leading board development

The Chair can be instrumental in encouraging the board to seek development that will improve its strategic ability. A strategically aware Chair brings a personal commitment to good governance based on the board's leadership. His/her relationship with the Chief Executive puts the Chair in a unique position to see the importance of board strategy to the management of the organisation. To make the most of board engagement, s/he can help the group improve by leading the drive toward development, suggesting development plans, appointing a committee to look into development options or simply helping the group understand how development could help.

Providing for Chair succession

By providing for the future, a good Chair helps support the strategic goals of the organisation and the strategic activity of the Chief Executive. Every organisation should have a Chair succession plan in place, and every Chair should personally see to it that there is procedure for selecting and preparing the person who will follow in his/her footsteps. Chair selection is a strategic act, providing an opportunity to find a person with the skills and abilities to lead the board as it needs to be led. It is a duty to the board, and also to the Chief Executive, who needs to know that s/he will have a Chair to work with.

Model documents for the role of Chair

The following Chair job description and person specification are designed to give organisations a clearer idea of what these important documents should look like. They are only templates: to serve to your organisation, your board must adapt them through a process of discussion and decision-making. The serving Chair can provide insights into the reality of the role. Both job description and person specification should be reviewed and revised periodically to keep up with changing organisational needs (there is a version for photocopying purposes on pages 49 and 50 of the *Resources* section).

Chair job description

Responsibilities as a trustee

- The Chair will continue to fulfil all those duties and responsibilities he/she assumed when he/she became a trustee.

- The Chair will abide by the Trustee Code of Conduct.

- The Chair will act in accordance with any additional organisational policies relating to trustee activity.

General Chair responsibilities

Providing leadership for the board as it fulfils its governance duties and responsibilities toward the organisation including:

- setting vision, values, mission, strategy and high-level policy in accordance with charity regulations and the governing document;

- monitoring the organisation's performance against established targets;

- securing financial stability for the organisation;

- protecting and managing organisational property and investments;

- safeguarding the organisation's reputation and values;

- making sure all organisational activities comply with regulations and the law;

- reviewing major risks and making provisions for the organisation to respond appropriately;

- appointing and managing the Chief Executive Officer (Chief Executive);

- organising and leading board development activities such as self-assessments;

- delegating the above duties appropriately.

Specific duties

Meetings

- **Planning meeting schedules and setting agendas:** The Chair establishes dates, times and locations of meetings and sets meeting agendas according to board procedures.

- **Leading meetings:** The Chair leads meetings and facilitates discussion, encouraging all trustees to participate and preventing more talkative members from dominating the debate.

- **Keeping trustees informed:** The Chair establishes and monitors systems for distributing information before meetings and keeping trustees updated between meetings.

- **Acting as a point of contact between meetings:** The Chair makes him/herself available to trustees and others for contact between meetings.

Board leadership

- **Building the board:** The Chair leads trustee recruitment and induction, strengthening the group by finding capable new trustees and providing for Chair succession.

- **Engaging the whole board:** The Chair uses the skills and interests of all board members and does not allow cliques or inner circles to form.

- **Developing governance effectiveness:** The Chair improves overall board effectiveness by taking steps to increase governance ability in the group and in individual trustees.
- **Seeking self-development:** The Chair seeks to improve governance practice by continually seeking to improve his or her own performance. S/he encourages feedback and responds appropriately.

- **Overseeing the work of committees:** The Chair oversees the establishment and activities of board committees, ensuring that they are accountable and report properly to the board.

- **Dealing with conflict on the board:** The Chair monitors and addresses conflict among board members and between trustees and other parts of the organisation.

Policy

- **Giving direction to board policy-making:** The Chair exercises leadership by setting priorities for the board and steering discussion toward strategic issues.

- **Monitoring the implementation of board decisions:** The Chair ensures that board decisions are communicated and implemented properly.

Representing the organisation

- **Acting as a spokesperson for the organisation:** The Chair speaks for the organisation when authorised.

- **Representing the organisation:** The Chair represents the organisation at public gatherings when asked.

Where staff are employed

- **Coordinating board management of the Chief Executive:** The Chair leads the board as it fulfils its management responsibilities toward the Chief Executive, overseeing role definition, selection, contracting, training, assessment and discipline.

- **Working with the Chief Executive Officer:** The Chair works with the Chief Executive on behalf of the board, coordinating efforts between the governing body and the executive. The Chair meets regularly with the Chief Executive to discuss strategic issues. S/he leads Chief Executive assessment, provides feedback, supports the Chief Executive and offers him/her appropriate development opportunities.

- **Developing the board with the Chief Executive:** Together the Chief Executive and Chair seek ways to improve board effectiveness by identifying development opportunities for the board and for the Chair.

- **Addressing conflict in the organisation:** The Chair monitors conflict in the organisation. He or she is available to help the Chief Executive, staff, trustees and others resolve conflicts. He or she takes steps to address conflict, acting to protect the organisation's reputation and preserve morale.

- **Sitting on appointment and disciplinary panels:** The Chair represents the board on appointment and disciplinary panels, especially those for the Chief Executive Officer.

Chair person specification

Essentials

Commitment to the organisation
Understanding of the legal duties, responsibilities and liabilities of trusteeship
Willingness to put time and effort into the Chair role
Respected and trusted by other board members

Personal qualities

Good, independent judgement
Impartiality, fairness and confidentiality
Willingness to speak his or her mind
Tact and diplomacy
Respect for others
Willingness to learn new skills

Specific abilities

Strategic vision
Creative thinking
Leading meetings
Working effectively as a team member
Good communication and interpersonal skills

Experience

Previous chairing experience (preferred but not required)
Previous leadership position
Experience of committee work

Role of the Chief Executive

The role of the Chief Executive is in many ways more familiar than that of the Chair. Just like executives in the private sector, he or she is a management professional with specific responsibilities laid out in his or her contract. Some typical responsibilities are: putting a strategic plan in place; protecting the financial health of the organisation; ensuring constitutional, legal and regulatory obligations are met; managing staff and so on. See the model Chief Executive job description and person specification at the end of this section for a more complete overview of the duties and tasks of the Chief Executive.

Since all organisations are different, it stands to reason that the role of the Chief Executive will vary from one organisation to the next. There is a wide spectrum of acceptable practice when it comes to Chief Executive activity and organisations can suit themselves as long as their arrangements conform to their governing document and legal requirements. However, it is essential that organisations define the Chief Executive role clearly and commit this definition to written policy. Clear Chief Executive role policy is fundamental to many aspects of good governance, not least establishing effective working relations between the Chair and the Chief Executive.

Defining the role: a task for the trustee board

The trustee board is responsible for defining the Chief Executive role. It does so by creating a framework of policy to guide and manage the organisation's top employee. The most important of these policies are the Chief Executive job description and person specification. Although many organisations manage without these documents, all organisations – and Chief Executives – can benefit from the clarity they bring.

Indeed, the Chief Executive job description and person specification are strategic documents with the power to shape the organisation on a profound level. They can be used to support governance strategies (such as strengthening Chief Executive/Chair cooperation) by asking for specific skills or experience and committing the Chief Executive to important goals. As such, they should be reviewed regularly in light of the organisation's long-term aims and kept up to date by the board. The serving Chief Executive can give valuable input to board deliberation, injecting a sense of realism into discussions about the role.

12 core Chief Executive responsibilities

1 backing the mission

2 modelling high ethical standards

3 leading management and staff

4 exercising financial stewardship

5 managing fundraising activity

6 ensuring accountability and compliance with the law

7 engaging the board in strategic thinking, planning and leadership

8 developing future leadership

9 nurturing external relations

10 serving as spokesperson and advocate

11 ensuring the effectiveness of programmes

12 supporting and developing the board and Chair

For more on strategies for defining the Chief Executive role and writing Chief Executive job descriptions and person specifications, see Dorothy Dalton's detailed guide, Recruiting a new Chief Executive, available from NCVO.

Other useful policies

Along with the job description and person specification, the trustee board should establish other core policies to help define the Chief Executive role. A Chief Executive code of conduct, popular in the private sector, is now becoming standard in the voluntary and community sector too. By communicating board expectations about behaviour, such codes help Chief Executives meet expectations and uphold standards. Such a code may include specific guidance about how to behave toward the Chair, thus shaping that relationship for the better.

Other key guidance for Chief Executive role clarity includes such organisation-wide policies as those on human resources, dealing with the media and communications. The board may also consider writing more detailed policy for the Chief Executive, such as a policy on Chief Executive/Chair relations. All of these board-authored policies will contribute to the executive's understanding of the role, strengthening good practice by bringing clarity.

The Chief Executive and the board

In governance theory, there is a clear division of labour between board and Chief Executive: the board determines mission, vision and long-term objectives, acting as the strategic engine of the organisation; the Chief Executive, as the board's top employee, responds to board decisions, finding practical ways to translate them into day-to-day organisational activity.

In reality, the relationship between the Chief Executive and the board is much more complicated. In some organisations it is the Chief Executive who effectively makes all the strategic decisions while the board merely approves (rubber stamps) his or her plans. In still others, the board and Chief Executive operate in separate universes, with board activity seemingly unrelated to what management is doing. Both these scenarios model poor governance practice: the lack of properly defined roles leads to poor accountability and can put the organisation at risk.

Yet even in healthy organisations, it's common for the governing board to rely heavily on the Chief Executive for guidance and advice. This makes sense: a competent Chief Executive knows the voluntary and community sector, keeps apace with changes, and brings valuable insights into how the organisation needs to develop in order to protect itself and thrive. This professional expertise is invaluable to a governing body that may be made up of individuals who don't have such a high level of practical know-how.

For this reason, the Chief Executive is a hugely influential figure in the realm of governance, even though he or she is not actually a member of the governing body. The challenge for boards is to find the best way to tap into Chief Executive expertise without compromising governance integrity. The challenge for the Chief Executive is to persuade the board to respond to the realities facing the organisation without stepping over the governance line. Part of the answer to this challenge lies with the

Chair: a trustee with extra responsibilities and the ability to act simultaneously as a buffer and medium for the relationship between the Chief Executive and board.

A Chief Executive's guide to making the most of your board

- Cultivate a positive attitude toward the board.
- Put aside time out of your busy schedule for working with the board.
- Bring human skills to your dealings with the board: sensitivity, tact and a willingness to listen.
- Take initiatives to the board in the first stages of the development process: let them have input before firm plans are put in place.
- Help the board feel satisfaction and a sense of ownership about the organisation's work.
- Develop your own knowledge of board leadership and governance practice.
- Let staff and senior managers know you think the board's role is vital.
- Attend to communication quality and systems: both are essential to keeping relations healthy.
- Pay close attention to your relationship with the Chair.
- View your own evaluation as an opportunity to strengthen your working relationship with the board.

Working with the Chair

For Chief Executives, the Chair is the key to the board. He or she is at once the Chief Executive's manager and a partner in organisational leadership. As any experienced Chief Executive will tell you, the Chair can be a help or a hindrance. There are good Chairs who offer the Chief Executive the benefit of their wisdom and support. They work hard, lending a hand with the board, providing a confidential shoulder to cry on and sticking their necks out to improve the organisation, even when the going gets tough. For Chief Executives, a good Chair is worth his or her weight in gold.

And then there are bad Chairs: obstructive, meddlesome, antagonistic, territorial, incompetent or just plain clueless. Whatever the issue with a poor Chair, his or her lack of cooperation or ability makes things much harder for the Chief Executive. Even the pushover Chair, the one who always does the executive's bidding without question, presents the Chief Executive with a problem of accountability. Given that the executive can't select his or her Chair, the Chief Executive needs to put effort into making the partnership work.

Making the Chair a priority

See an effective partnership with the Chair as important to your job. Don't forget that the Chair represents the board, the body that ultimately takes responsibility for everything you do. Set aside time to make yourself available to the Chair. Have regular, scheduled meetings and encourage casual contact between meetings, within reason. Take the Chair's calls. Answer questions fully and respectfully. Show an interest in the work the Chair is doing and be generous with advice when asked.

Tapping into the Chair's expertise

The Chair knows things about the organisation you don't know. Tap into the Chair's expertise by learning more about his or her experience in the organisation and on the board. Find out about the Chair's background and his or her reasons for wanting to serve the organisation. Discover more about the board group from the Chair: those insights into personalities and attitudes can make all the difference to planning a convincing presentation. Use the Chair to test-drive explanations: if you can make the Chair understand you, then you stand a better chance with the group. Ask the Chair to act as your Devil's Advocate, throwing up objections s/he thinks the board will raise. Adopt the Chair's suggestions as to the best approach.

Being supportive

The Chair needs your help, too. The Chair's job is difficult and many individuals find themselves in the role with no training and no previous experience. Your knowledge and skills can be very useful to your Chair. So can your awareness of good governance practice. Make a point of listening to your Chair and sharing his or her concerns. Look for ways to offer support, either moral or material. Be willing to teach him or her skills when you can, such as how to read a financial statement. Suggest appropriate training or mentoring programmes and point the Chair toward useful publications and websites, such as NCVO's. Help your Chair think of alternative strategies to stubborn problems. Act as a sounding board.

Encouraging good practice

Although not a member of the trustee board, the Chief Executive is an influential voice in governance and can encourage the board to set up good systems for selecting, inducting, and training the Chair such as those recommended by this guide. Tact is needed when making suggestions: avoid the appearance of criticising the serving Chair. Work one-on-one with the Chair first, introducing new ideas, and then, together, present the concepts to the whole board.

'Build a strong professional relationship with your Chair in which both of you understand your different but complementary roles. Nurture and cultivate all your trustees. However busy you are, make sure that you put aside time for building and developing these relationships. Remember, their role is not to rubber stamp everything you want, but to be a challenging friend. They have ultimate responsibility for the charity. It is a key part of your role to ensure that they fulfil this responsibility. Have sufficient confidence in yourself to give the board an accurate and balanced picture of what is going on. Give them both the good and the bad news. If you have difficulties with your trustees, seek advice and help and do not try to turn the senior management team or other employees against them. Maintain high standards of professionalism throughout.'

From *Recruiting a New Chief Executive* by Dorothy Dalton, NCVO Publications

Developing the Chair and board

The Chief Executive can help persuade the board to improve its skills. With his or her perspective as head of management and partner in strategic governance, the Chief Executive is in a good position to see the value of training and development activities and to communicate this vision to the board. Working with the Chair, the Chief Executive can suggest development strategies, present options, assist board development committees and participate alongside trustees in activities, such as role training, retreats and away-days.

The Chief Executive also has a role in developing the Chair. As Chair's partner, the Chief Executive can help him or her identify places where skills need strengthening. An all-board assessment should include a special Chair assessment, and this can provide a starting point for creating a programme of Chair development. The Chief Executive can also lend a hand by coaching the Chair in areas such as interpreting financial statements and understanding operational issues. For more on developing the Chair and board, see Making the most of shared responsibilities.

Model documents for the role of Chief Executive

The following Chief Executive job description and person specification are designed to give organisations a clearer idea of what these important documents should look like. They are only templates: to serve to your organisation, the trustee board needs to adapt them through a process of discussion and decision-making. The serving Chief Executive can provide insights into the reality of the role. Both job description and person specification should be reviewed and revised periodically to keep up with changing organisational needs (there is a version for photocopying purposes on pages 51 and 52 of the *Resources* section).

Chief Executive job description

General responsibilities

Providing leadership to the organisation and to take responsibility for its management and administration within the strategic and accountability frameworks established by the board of trustees.

With the Chair, enabling the board of trustees to fulfil its duties and responsibilities for the proper governance of the organisation and to see to it that the board receives advice and information in a timely, thorough and appropriate manner.

Specific Duties

Working with the board

- With the Chair, seeing to it that the board of trustees formulates and regularly reviews the organisation's vision, mission and values;

- In partnership with trustees, developing a long-term strategy for the organisation within the vision, mission and values established by the board;
- With the Chair, ensuring that the board can adequately monitor annual plans, targets and performance;

- Reporting to the board on organisational progress, providing information and answering for organisational performance;

- With the Chair, developing policy proposals for board discussion and decision;

- With the Chair, establishing the annual calendar for board and subcommittee meetings;

- Supporting the Chair, suggesting development opportunities as appropriate;

- Enabling the board to broaden its capabilities and develop its leadership potential.

Leading and managing the organisation

- Ensuring that a long-term strategy is in place to guide the organisation in achieving its objectives;

- Being responsible to trustees for the overall financial health of the organisation;

- Ensuring that the organisation has the human, material and financial resources it needs to operate effectively;

- Seeking out and developing new strategies for ensuring future resources;

- Taking appropriate steps to protect the organisation from risk;

- Seeing to it that the organisation fulfils its constitutional, regulatory and legal obligations;

- Ensuring that the organisation has the right management systems and structures to carry out its work effectively, accountably and safely;

- Providing leadership to the management team and direction to all staff;

- Ensuring that staff, volunteers and others working in the organisation are focussed on achieving the mission and strategic priorities.

Promoting the organisation

- Protecting and enhancing the reputation of the organisation;

- Seeking opportunities to expand and promote awareness of the organisation's work;

- Using the media appropriately to raise the organisation's profile:

- Acting as spokesperson when authorised;

- Assisting in the formulation of marketing strategies and campaigns;

- Ensuring that marketing materials and other communications accurately and persuasively present the vision, mission and values of the organisation;

- Cooperating with fundraising staff, advising on grants, taking part in campaigns and meeting funders when necessary;

- Overseeing the regular updating of the website, production of the newsletter and other communications with supporters.

Chief Executive person specification

Essentials

- Commitment to the organisation's vision, values and mission

- Personal integrity and credibility

- Commitment to self-development

- Dedication to developing the organisation

Personal qualities

- Charisma

- Tact

- Responsiveness

- Realism

- Honesty

- Enthusiasm

Specific abilities

- Financial and management expertise

- Content and programme expertise

- Excellent communication and people skills

- Ability to build networks and make connections

- Strategic orientation

- Ability to take the lead

- Team player

Experience

- Track record of general management at the senior executive level

- Proven ability to work successfully with a trustee board

- Experience in managing an organisation of comparable size

- Knowledge of voluntary and community sector governance practice

Built-in tensions

It's not your imagination: there are inherent stresses between the roles of Chief Executive and Chair. Understanding these conflicting pressures can help unlock the potential for partnership.

Chief Executives and Chairs have different demands on them

Chief Executives are busy, stressed people working in a highly charged, highly responsive and demanding environment. Some are dealing with high level political issues, vulnerable people, or crises that call for fast responses. Chairs are frequently (but by no means always) semi-retired or retired with more time for detail. Chief Executives may be reluctant to make time for the Chair if the Chair seems preoccupied with less important issues. But Chief Executives welcome a constructive, critical friend to help them cope with the many demands they face.

Chief Executives and Chairs are similar kinds of people

Many Chairs have been Chief Executives in the past. With the best intentions, such Chairs tend to share the executive perspective and try to bring a management focus to what should be a governance role. They know how to lead from the front, but lack experience with their new, very different position in the organisation. Their inclination is to go on doing what they do well – managing – when they should be developing the board and supporting the Chief Executive. To get over this hurdle, Chairs need specific training in their new role.

Chief Executives and Chairs have different definitions of success

Chief Executives and Chairs who have not set out specific goals for their partnership may well end up working toward different goals. Because their jobs are so different, they may develop conflicting definitions of what a successful partnership means. As a result, they may find themselves working against one another or in an uncoordinated way. A shared vision, good guidance from the organisation and a working agreement all help turn inherent difference into a positive factor.

Chief Executives and Chairs go wrong without guidance

The natural tensions between Chief Executives and Chairs are exacerbated by a lack of direction from the organisation. In a vacuum of conscious policy or a vision of what Chief Executive/Chair relations should be, the partners may well establish an adversarial, over-dependent or otherwise dysfunctional way of working together. The board needs to offer pragmatic, realistic guidance to help them find their way.

Part 1

Relationship profiles

Every relationship is different; relationships between Chairs and Chief Executives are no exception. Much depends on individual personalities and the special circumstances that face the organisation. Yet healthy, functional Chief Executive/Chair relationships have characteristics in common and it's possible to build a model of how a good relationship functions in the context of good governance practice.

Portrait of a partnership

Both Chief Executive and Chair selected by the board with the help of a carefully thought-out job description and person specification. Time is taken over the choice in an effort to make sure that the two individuals have complementary skills and working styles. Both are experienced: Chief Executive in management, the Chair in governance and communication. Both receive a suitable induction to the role that involves their opposite number.

With a grounding provided by good selection and induction processes, the Chief Executive and Chair begin their working relationship by establishing a working agreement that lays out the terms of their partnership. They may also be guided by board-authored policies that give detailed instruction on certain aspects of their partnership. At all times, their work together conforms to organisational vision, supports mission and reflects values established by the governing board.

Chief Executive and Chair hold regular, scheduled meetings at times and places convenient to both parties. Before the meeting, both prepare to an agreed standard. However, the meeting format is flexible enough to allow them to be spontaneous and say the things they need to say. Meetings are treated confidentially but are documented. Others can attend the meeting when appropriate but the Chief Executive and Chair are able to meet privately, too. Special preparatory meetings may take place before events, such as the AGM, or in advance of board meetings where very important proposals will be tabled. The Chief Executive and Chair make time for one another between meetings as well, communicating freely and sharing information.

The tone of the communication at and between meetings is cordial, professional and respectful. Chief Executive and Chair come together as equals, each responsible for leading a part of the organisation, jointly responsible for providing strategic leadership to the organisation as a whole. Relations are friendly but not too cosy. There is room for constructive criticism on both sides. There is also room for both parties to seek support, offer advice, and provide a confidential ear when needed.

Chief Executive/Chair meetings focus on issues of strategic importance to the organisation. The Chair attends on behalf of the governing board. In meetings with the Chief Executive, s/he is the board's eyes and ears, seeking clarification from the executive and striving to learn the reason behind management actions or recommendations.

The Chair brings the governance perspective to the meeting, maintaining an emphasis on vision, values and mission that balances the Chief Executive's inevitable preoccupation with making things run on a practical level. With his/her superior knowledge of the board, its individual members and dynamics, the Chair is a valuable sounding board for the Chief Executive, offering insight into board attitudes and advice on how to present proposals effectively. When giving the Chief Executive feedback, the Chair always uses tact and consideration.

The Chief Executive sees the Chair as a partner, a resource of governance insight and an important interface with the board. He or she works with the Chair to develop proposals to put before the board, using the Chair's insider knowledge to find the right approach. By helping the Chair understand the practical necessities thrown up by organisational strategy, the Chief Executive strengthens the ability of the Chair to act as a true partner. He or she is honest with the Chair, and does not withhold information, especially about bad news. With staff, especially senior managers, the Chief Executive stresses the importance of the board's role in the organisation.

Development is an important point where Chief Executive and Chair come together. The Chair is sensitive to the development needs of the Chief Executive and ready to suggest development opportunities. He or she is willing to go to bat for Chief Executive development, bringing arguments to persuade a (sometimes) reluctant board to invest in their senior executive. Similarly, the Chief Executive has an eye out for ways to develop the Chair and the board and s/he brings her ideas to the Chair for discussion. The two should collaborate on finding ways to improve board practice and in convincing the board to seek development or to create needed policy. When appropriate, they can participate in development activities together.

The Chair and Chief Executive work together to promote organisational policy and projects, appearing in public and at board meetings to speak about issues. As spokespeople, both leaders play to their strengths, using the operational and governance arguments to support decisions or urge action. They always show mutual support in public, having worked out any differences in private beforehand.

Patterns in different organisations

The Charity Commission, NCVO and ACEVO have all uncovered evidence that Chief Executive/Chair relationships fall into patterns depending on the size and level of development of the organisation.

Large

Systems and processes are well developed in large organisations and there is usually enough staff so that the Chair and Chief Executive can concentrate on their most important tasks. Clear roles are more important than ever. Chair and Chief Executive both need to know the systems and processes by heart: their leadership and authority rely on it. They need to work together to make sure that things are done correctly that new processes and systems are established when necessary. In large organisations, the Chief Executive and Chair roles emphasise coordination. At the same time, the organisation is more set in its ways and there is a danger becoming too institutionalised, going stale, losing touch. Chief Executives and Chairs need to work together to keep things fresh and the mission in the foreground, questioning old ways when necessary and backing one another up when the time has come to introduce change.

Medium

The findings of the NCVO Almanac 2006 show that Chief Executives and Chairs in medium sized voluntary and community sector organisations are feeling the most pressure. These organisations are squeezed on both sides by scarce funds and the need to compete with other organisations to survive. The Chief Executive/Chair partnership is stressed by a host of demands: protecting the organisation from risk, finding resources, developing organisational identity and pursuing the mission. Both need leadership skills in spades. The partnership needs to work together to establish and implement good systems–more and more of these as the organisation gets bigger. The Chief Executive/Chair duo needs to be pragmatic and visionary at the same time. Strategy becomes ever more important and both partners need to hone their strategic know-how. More than ever before, Chief Executives and Chairs need to help one another by seeking development opportunities for each other and looking for ways to strengthen their work together. They need to be flexible, both individually and as a team, and they need to show adaptability–and bring that spirit of adaptability to the organisation.

Small

Chief Executives and Chairs assure us that small is still beautiful when it comes to organisations. Close to the grass roots where the mission comes from, small organisations often enjoy a clarity of purpose and dedication that evades larger, more bureaucratic organisations. Typically, the Chair and members of the board will still be involved in delivering services. Everyone wears more than one hat. For those organisations developed enough to have a professional executive it can be a challenge for trustees, especially the Chair, to stand back and let this professional do what s/he has been hired to do. Taking on the first member of staff is a milestone for organisations that changes the role of the board forever and usually calls for a new ways of working. The Chair will closely supervise the executive and possibly other workers as well. The leadership (board, Chair, executive) need to pay special attention to handling volunteers at this point: they are essential to the organisation. A big challenge for those leading the organisation is providing for the future. They need to decide whether the organisation will grow or stay the same size. And they need to decide what agenda should be used to shape the organisation in the future.

When the partners aren't equal

Experienced Chief Executive/new Chair

Most Chief Executives will work with more than one Chair during their tenure, so this is a common situation. Good selection and induction systems in which the Chief Executive participates can help pave the way toward a good working relationship. The Chief Executive is in a position to either help or hinder his new partner. A cooperative Chief Executive shares information openly, makes him- or herself available to the new Chair and actively looks for ways to help him/her learn the ropes. Development is one way to cultivate a skilled strategic partner. A good induction that includes specific training in chairing skills is a boon to any incoming Chair, even one with experience. It is also the time to declare a new beginning: if there have been problems with the Chair or board in the past, its time to wipe the slate clean. Learn from past mistakes and put measures in place to keep them from happening again. Both parties should be prepared to let the relationship change and develop as the new Chair gets more competent and independent.

Experienced Chair/new Chief Executive

This is the less common of the two scenarios. The Chair has a background with the organisation and knows the trustees, and the dynamics of the board as a group. Territoriality can be a danger, but much depends on how the new Chief Executive is brought in. Recruitment and selection systems that involve the board encourage ownership of the decision to hire the executive and promote cooperation once s/he steps into the new role. Frequently, a new Chief Executive comes in with a new mandate. Depending on his/her attitude toward the new recruit, the Chair can either support the mandate or try to squash it. If all is well with the way the new Chief Executive arrives, then the Chair can be a huge help as the Chief Executive finds his/her feet. The Chair is a key figure in an induction process, bringing insight into board attitudes and governance matters. It is a good idea for the Chair to get familiar with the skills and abilities as well as the personality of his/her new partner, and to think about how the organisation can best put these to use. The Chair should also be on the lookout for ways to support the Chief Executive by offering training or suggesting a coaching or mentoring scheme.

Building healthy partnerships

Establishing core policies

These short, seemingly simple policy statements have a profound effect on the organisation and provide a firm foundation for establishing other policies and systems to support the Chief Executive/Chair partnership.

Vision

The governing board needs to create a vision statement, a three- or four-sentence policy that paints a picture of the world as the organisation would like it to be. Activities such as retreats, away days and special board meetings provide an opportunity for boards to work on vision and devise strategies for communicating that vision throughout the organisation. The Chair will naturally participate along with the board, but the Chief Executive should also take part, thus giving leaders the opportunity to forge a shared sense of purpose.

Mission

For the Chief Executive and Chair, the mission is a touchstone that influences all their work together. A powerful cohesive force in the organisation, mission is also a point of basic agreement between its key leaders. Mission provides a clear objective against which to measure the effectiveness of their partnership: 'Are we serving the mission?' At the same time, a dysfunctional Chair/Chief Executive relationship can present risks that put the mission in jeopardy. Mission should be on the lips of Chief Executives and Chairs and a guiding force in their work together.

Values

A board-authored statement of values gives everyone including the Chief Executive and Chair something to base their activity on. This broad statement lays out qualities the organisation strives to uphold in all it does. It is useful as a reference when making policy and when determining specific guidelines for interpersonal relations such as the Chief Executive/Chair partnership.

Chair and Chief Executive selection

Good recruitment, selection and induction systems for both the Chair and the Chief Executive lay the groundwork for a solid working relationship.

Selecting a Chair who can partner the Chief Executive

Good practice recommends that all organisations establish written procedures for replacing the Chair, even in organisations that do not anticipate a change of Chairs in the near future. Selecting a Chair offers an opportunity to review the role of the Chair in the organisation and to address the needs of the board for a leader and, as importantly, of the Chief Executive for a strategic partner. Whether the new Chair is selected from among existing trustees or recruited through a wide-ranging search outside the organisation, the ability to work with the Chief Executive is a key criterion. Candidates should be given specific instruction on what will be expected of them in as far as working with the Chief Executive goes.

Here, character and personal style can be as important as ability. Those making the appointment need to determine how well the new candidate will be able to cooperate with the Chief Executive and how much s/he will bring to the partnership. The ideal candidate will be a complement to the Chief Executive, providing support in the areas where the executive is less strong. At the same time, those selecting the Chair need to beware of sowing the seeds of conflict by choosing an individual who will clash with the Chief Executive. Intentionally setting these two leaders at odds is not a good way to ensure accountability or effectiveness. Cooperation, within an established governance structure, is the key.

To make sure this is the case, some organisations allow their Chief Executive to participate directly in the selection process. In others, the executive is allowed to advise the selection committee and have input into the Chair job description and person specification. The Chief Executive can also play an important part in the Chair induction process, helping the new board leader get up to speed as quickly as possible.

Recruiting a Chair-friendly Chief Executive

Chief Executive recruitment should always be carried out by the book: transparently, systematically and with the involvement of the trustee board at every stage. Recruitment should start with an up-to-date job description and a person specification for the role, authored by the board. This encourages a feeling of ownership for the process, and helps ensure that the incoming Chief Executive already has the board behind him/her. Additionally, he or she will know what the board expects in terms of cooperation with the Chair.

When searching for a new Chief Executive, organisations should obviously look for the best possible manager, but they should also take into account personality and an ability to work with the Chair and the board in a strategic partnership. There's little sense in choosing a dynamic autocrat to lead your organisation if what you really need is someone who is good at building consensus.

Recruitment committees and boards doing the search need to have clear criteria that will lead them to the right kinds of individuals. Here, the vision of the board for the organisation is vital for giving the right cues to hire the right person. The ability to cooperate and collaborate with the Chair and trustee board should come high on the list of desired qualities. The Chief Executive should also bring skills and abilities the organisation lacks. Finding a balance between these two things can be a challenge, but it can be done.

Part 3

Induction is a key time for establishing Chief Executive/Chair relations. The Chair should be involved in Chief Executive induction, offering the support and insight into governance matters that the Chief Executive needs to get up to speed.

Establishing the partnership

Chief Executives and Chairs face a steep learning curve as they begin their partnership. Hopefully, they will have a framework of policy such as organisational vision, mission and values to help them establish the working relationship. Specific policies on behaviour, such as job descriptions and codes of conduct, also act as touchstones, communicating standards and boundaries. Even with this guidance, much still comes down to the individuals involved. What they do in the early days will shape the partnership for the rest of the time they work together.

Making partnership a priority

New Chief Executive and Chair partners should meet face to face as soon as possible. Don't let months elapse before the new Chair is allowed to sit down with the Chief Executive! Schedule a meeting at the earliest opportunity. Both parties should expect to put in more time in the early stages of the partnership to establish working practices and get to know their opposite number. The Chief Executive especially needs to make this a priority. The trustee board should make it clear that it expects its executive to make time for the Chair.

The beginning of a partnership is a great time to offer both the Chief Executive and Chair development and training to support their joint venture. Governance and role training are especially valuable at this point. On a smaller scale, it can be worthwhile to hire a professional facilitator to help the Chief Executive and Chair have the conversations they need to have to set out their working practices.

Determining working styles

Chief Executives and Chairs may be very different sorts of people, research shows. They often have different backgrounds and experience. Their areas of expertise differ and so do their preferred styles of working. This difference can be an advantage for organisations, bringing a broader range of skills and abilities to leadership roles, provided it is handled well.

To improve cooperation, Chief Executive/Chair pairs can seek help in the form of personality profile tests, like the popular DiSC assessment, that give insight into how individuals think and work. Professionally facilitated discussions focusing on work patterns and preferences can also shed light on the source of a lack of coordination. The information revealed by such exercises is useful as Chief Executives and Chairs formulate their working agreement (see below).

Forming a Chief Executive/Chair working agreement

There are many factors shaping the Chief Executive/Chair relationship including board policies, codes of conduct and, don't forget, the law. Yet the agreement these two individuals make with one another remains a powerful tool for fostering good working relations. Such an agreement should be a simple affair, established together and approved by the trustee board. It should cover the following issues:

Where and when to meet

The place and time should be convenient for both parties.

How often to meet

Meetings should be scheduled and regular. It's a good idea to hold an additional Chief Executive/Chair meeting to prepare for a special board meeting or AGM.

Meeting preparation

What preparation should both parties do before the meeting? Will there be pre-meeting information to review?

Sharing information

What information do you expect to get from one another? What media will you use to convey information? (post, email, telephone)

Access between meetings

Chief Executive and Chair should try to make themselves available to one another between meetings. Set guidelines for when to contact one another and lay out expectations for responding.

Pet peeves

Seemingly trivial things can matter a lot: Chief Executive and Chair should lay out their preferences honestly.

Religious observance issues

Be up front about religious matters when they affect the meetings and scheduling.

Boundaries

Both the Chair and the Chief Executive will deal with matters that require confidentiality. Map out areas and issues you can't talk about for reasons of confidentiality.

Breaks and holidays

Both partners should take breaks and holidays. (This is especially important for Chief Executives, since many executives never take time off and need to be encouraged by their Chair partner to do so.) Discuss when these will take place and how decisions are to be handled while one or both partners are away.

Dos and Don'ts for maintaining good working relations

DO

- Make a working agreement and respect it.
- Hold regular, scheduled meetings.
- Provide role training for both partners.
- Agree on who will speak for the organisation in what circumstances.
- Seek mediation and facilitation support to help overcome conflicts.
- Return to first principles: review vision, values, mission and strategic aims together.

DON'T

- Withhold vital information, especially if it's bad news.
- Spring surprises on one another at meetings or in public.
- Break confidences or gossip about each other.
- Ignore policies for communicating and working with other members of staff.
- Deliberately act in an adversarial or provocative way.
- Cut off communication.

Part 3

Improving communication

Communication is absolutely fundamental to the success of the Chief Executive/Chair relationship. Their partnership acts a primary conduit for information between the governing body and the executive. If this conduit is blocked–for example as a result of conflict, role confusion, personal mistrust or a lack of adequate systems–then neither the Chief Executive nor the board can function optimally. In fact, so much depends on Chief Executive/Chair communication that organisations should be prepared to devote both time and resources toward developing the skills and processes that will make good communication a matter of course.

Supporting communication through policy

Chief Executive/Chair communication is a small but important element in the communication activity of any organisation. Because communication is a strategic value for any organisation, the governing board, lead by the Chair, must establish a raft of policies to guide communication practice throughout the organisation. These communication policies help protect the organisation from a host of risks associated with poor communication practice and they provide the Chief Executive and Chair with a starting point for developing communication practice.

For more detailed information on establishing organisational communication systems see *Better communication = better governance?* by Tesse Akpeki and Tess Woodcraft, available from NCVO.

Framework policies to support communication

The trustee board can begin the task of supporting Chief Executive/Chair communication by providing general communication guidance for the whole organisation.

Communication values

The board needs to make a written policy that sets out the values to shape all communication. The policy may use terms like 'honest, respectful, responsive, compassionate, prompt.'

Communication style

Style itself sends a message and organisational communication style should be a deliberate choice. The board needs to establish general guidelines on style for the organisation. This style will shape all communication decisions and policies, including those regarding the Chief Executive and Chair.

Human resources and communication

Every organisation needs a comprehensive human resources policy setting forth standards, protocols and requirements for the treatment of people at every level and in every circumstance. Specific guidance on how communication will be handled should form part of that policy.

Media

In this day and age, every organisation needs a policy that states how it will handle the media and the public. Such a policy forms part of an overall media strategy that helps the organisation manage its public profile and protect its reputation. For the Chair and Chief Executive, dealing with the media is an important matter. It can also be a source of conflict, especially when one or the other speaks out of turn on organisational business in public.

Specific board/staff communication policies

Many problems that arise between trustee boards and staff including the Chief Executive arise over miscommunication: a staff member brings a complaint to a trustee, circumventing the Chief Executive; a key committee member gives instructions to staff regarding a programme or service without advising the Chair or management.

Such situations can be avoided by establishing clear protocols on communications between trustees (including the Chair) and staff members (including the Chief Executive). These should provide detailed guidance about the right way for trustees to interact with staff, about when and how to air complaints and about how to handle confidential board matters with staff. As a general rule, all significant communication or work with staff members should be cleared with the Chief Executive beforehand.

Specific policies on Chief Executive/Chair communications

Depending on how much control it feels it needs to exert over relations between its top leaders, the trustee board may choose to make policy that deals specifically with Chief Executive/Chair relations. Such a policy might lay out how often the two are to meet, how communication is to be documented and how both parties will communicate with the board. It's best to involve both the Chief Executive and the Chair in formulating such a policy or let them put together the initial draft for the board to review and discuss.

Discussion exercise
Ask your opposite number the following questions:

- What is keeping you awake at night?
- How is this problem strategically important to our organisation?
- How does it (or could it) affect our mission?
- What can I do to help you deal with this problem?
- What would make you feel more confident and optimistic?

Codes of conduct

Trustee code of conduct

Trustee codes of conduct work for the good of boards and organisations in many ways and they form an important part of a total plan to encourage good communication throughout the organisation.

For more on establishing a trustee code of conduct see NCVO's publication *Best behaviour: using trustee codes of conduct to improve governance practice* by Tesse Akpeki.

Specific code additions for the Chair

As a trustee, the Chair is bound by the trustee code of conduct to uphold good standards of behaviour in all s/he does. This may provide enough guidance for the Chair when it comes to working with the Chief Executive, or the board may think it advisable to provide more specific guidance to the Chair regarding behaviour. The board should set any additional guidance down in policy form, avoiding putting so many restrictions on Chair/Chief Executive interaction that the two find it hard to meet and deal with one another in a normal way.

A code of conduct for the Chief Executive

The Chief Executive will naturally be bound by the agreement s/he makes with the trustee board at the time of appointment. S/he will be further guided by general board policies on organisational values, communication, human resources and so on. However, a Chief Executive code of conduct allows the trustee board to be more specific about the executive's expected behaviour, and especially to be explicit about the things s/he is expected NOT to do, for example limits on power and prohibitions. A negative approach to a code of conduct protects the organisation and leaves the executive freedom to work effectively.

Cultivating the art of strategic communication

Much rides on the quality and timeliness Chief Executive/Chair communication. The challenge for Chief Executive/Chair partners is to have the right conversations at the right time. This sounds simple, but experienced Chief Executives and Chairs will be quick to point out how difficult it can be. Good systems such as those mentioned in this guide can help Chief Executives and Chairs frame conversations and say the things they need to say in a useful way. But both leaders need to develop an awareness of what a strategic conversation is, and then apply patience and persistence to making those conversations happen in the context of their partnership.

Fortunately, both partners can get practical help in strengthening communication skills. Communication development strategies include:

- expert coaching

- peer mentoring

- professionally facilitated model meetings

- media training

- diversity training

Communicating the strategic vision together

Chief Executives and Chairs are partners in leadership for the organisation. One of their key tasks is communicating their shared vision to the rest of the organisation. The following are steps they may take to achieve this:

- coordinating their efforts as spokespeople for the organisation to the media and public so that they are in agreement;

- using media such as the organisation's website or newsletter to address organisational issues in tandem;

- co-presenting proposals or information at board meetings with the Chair speaking for governance and the Chief Executive for operations;

- appearing together at the AGM to present important items;

- supporting fundraising efforts by speaking with funders and offering their expertise to fundraisers.

Chief Executive/Chair communication basics

- Make sure your communications are consistent with other organisational policies including codes of conduct.

- Agree who will act as spokesperson for the organisation in a given circumstance. Check your decisions against organisational communication policy.

- Be up front about your communication preferences: if you want things in writing, say so.

- Be honest about bad news. Deliver it yourself and leave enough time for reactions and discussion. Try to work through problems together. Focus on solution strategies.

- Hold pre-meetings before board meetings, AGMs and other events where you will appear together. Decide how you will share the task of presenting information.

- Be explicit about confidentiality. If you don't want your partner to discuss something with others, say so. Come to an agreement about what confidentiality means.

- Respect personal preferences: religious holidays, appropriate and inappropriate jokes, jargon, good/bad times to call.

- Make pro-active strategies for joint communication on the website, in mailings and newsletters, to the media.

- Always debrief together: review what worked and what didn't and build learning into future work.

Part 3

Don't over-communicate. Copious communication is not necessarily effective. Instead, come to an understanding about what information you need to receive from one another and restrict communications to what is really necessary.

Exercise: 10-minute topics

- Set aside 10 minutes at your next Chief Executive/Chair meeting to discuss one of the following topics:
- What difference is our work making? How do we know?
- How do we currently support the board? How can we do more?
- How does this partnership help the Chief Executive deal with staff issues? What can we do to strengthen our support?
- Is our partnership style right for us? Is it right for the organisation?

Making the most of shared responsibilities

Chief Executives and Chairs have joint responsibility for some of the central jobs in government and leadership. The following are key areas where Chief Executives and Chairs can make the most of working together for the good of the organisation.

Engaging the board in strategy

The creation, communication and implementation of long-term strategy are central to the success of organisations and an important area where Chief Executive and Chair work together. While the question of strategy is a complicated one and different for every organisation, there are key points at which strategic planning brings Chair and Chief Executive together, offering opportunities to support one another and put strategy at the heart of governance.

Seeking early board involvement

Working with the Chair, the Chief Executive should get the board involved in strategic questions before problems have been framed or plans formed. The ratification of any plan by the board should be the end result of a longer process through which the board has influence over the content of the plan. Getting the board involved at the very earliest stages, long before plans are concretised or strategies determined, is the best way to get strategic input.

Planning an approach

The Chief Executive and Chair can work together to find the right way to approach the board with policy proposals. Using the Chief Executive's managerial knowledge and the Chair's knowledge of the board and governance issues, the pair should be able to come up with a presentation that encourages strategic engagement on the part of the board. Co-presenting proposals sends the message that the Chief Executive and Chair are of one mind about the importance of an issue.

Suggesting a governance review

A governance review can be an effective way to start the process of improving strategic engagement by the trustee board. The Chief Executive and Chair first need to educate themselves about governance reviews, what they entail, and whether they are right for their organisation. Once they feel they are sufficiently informed, the partners can find the best way of presenting the question to the board for discussion and decision.

Special activities

The Chief Executive and Chair can work together to find new ways to deepen board engagement through new kinds of activity. Away days, retreats and facilitated discussions give boards the opportunity to focus on issues and feed their views into the strategic process. Presentations by the Chief Executive and other managers provide valuable information from the practical side of the question and help trustees understand executive concerns.

Breaking bad news to the board: a Chief Executive's guide

- Go over the issues with the Chair in advance; jointly plan a presentation strategy.
- Offer a range of options, ideas and suggestions along with the bad news.
- Frame the bad news in terms of possible benefits, pros and cons.
- Frame the feedback you require from the board; tell them what you need.
- Lay out a time frame for decisions and action.

Improving board meetings

It is the Chair's responsibility to run board meetings. By working in partnership with the Chief Executive, the Chair can increase the value of meetings.

Collaborating on meeting agendas

By building agendas around strategic issues and scheduling board decisions to align with important funding deadlines or reporting dates, the Chair and Chief Executive can help the board work more effectively.

Creating a Chief Executive slot at every meeting

Allocating some time during every board meeting to the Chief Executive allows the executive to keep the board up to speed with organisational activity. It also gives trustees a chance to find out what's on the Chief Executive's mind and what support or direction s/he needs from them. For greatest success, define the aims of the Chief Executive session ahead of time. Strive to create supportive atmosphere. To avoid confusion, establish guidelines that set out times when the Chief Executive cannot be present at meetings, such as when the board is discussing his or her performance or remuneration.

Co-presenting important agenda items

The Chief Executive and Chair can make a persuasive double act at board meetings. This approach works best for presenting significant information, such as the results of an assessment, research findings, or a proposal for a new project or initiative. For best effects, the Chief Executive and Chair should agree about the way the information will be presented, settle on recommendations, when given, and work out their roles beforehand.

Seeking skill development for the Chair

The Chief Executive and Chair can work together to find appropriate development opportunities to strengthen the Chair's core skills: meeting planning, facilitation, leadership. See Chair appraisal and development for more details.

Chief Executive appraisal and development

The Chief Executive appraisal process offers an unparalleled opportunity for the Chief Executive and Chair to work together to strengthen governance and leadership. It goes without saying that the appraisal process should form part of regular assessment procedures and that all its terms should be agreed with the executive beforehand. The process itself must be transparent, fair and carried out with the participation and approval of the whole board. The criteria for assessment should be clear, measurable and linked to strategic goals. Feedback should be given in a way that has been agreed beforehand, and bonuses and other changes to remuneration awarded as agreed.

Because the appraisal process is so important, many organisations hire specialised human resources professionals to help them establish the right criteria and procedures. Many go farther, contracting consultants to help them perform the assessment and shape the feedback they offer to the Chief Executive. This is especially valuable in cases where the trustee board and Chair lack that management experience that will allow them to interpret how well the Chief Executive has really performed. Consultants can bring a level of expertise to the process not available within the organisation and can prove highly worthwhile.

Within this context, the Chair should make a point of offering positive as well as negative feedback to the Chief Executive. It is not the time to judge the Chief Executive on aspects of performance that were not originally part of the assessment criteria. Tact and sensitivity are needed on the part of the Chair when presenting findings. The Chief Executive should be given an opportunity to respond. Dialogue is essential to shaping the next cycle of appraisal and moving into the future.

Appraisal provides an opportunity to identify areas where the Chief Executive would benefit from development and the Chair should be on the lookout for ways to provide support. The Chief Executive him- or herself may have a clear idea of the kind of help s/he needs to improve performance and the trustee board should be willing to listen to requests. Outside human resource consultants and organisations such as NCVO and ACEVO offer guidance and services for developing executives (see Resources).

Crafting support for the Chief Executive

Don't know what help to offer your Chief Executive? Start by having conversations around specific tasks, functions or issues such as:

- benchmarking
- monitoring
- tricky membership issues
- working with managers
- dealing with funders
- time and priority management

Chair appraisal and development

Chair appraisal offers a way to support and develop the leader of the board. It's also an opportunity to confront performance issues that may be affecting governance and Chief Executive/Chair relations. It should form an integral part of board development and be carried out in the context of overall board assessment. Be advised that Chair appraisal is *not* recommended as a strategy for dealing with Chair performance problems in isolation. When the issue is only with the Chair, it's more effective to use alternative interventions such as those mentioned below.

Chair appraisal should be based on the written documents defining the role and expectations of the Chair including the Chair job description and person specification, the Chair code of conduct and other policies relating to the work of the Chair. Appraisal may be carried out using a form (such as that provided in *Good governance: the Chair's role* by Dorothy Dalton) or it may be conducted through one-to-one discussions. The Vice Chair or other trustee, an appropriate non-trustee with governance experience, a development professional or even the Chair of another organisation can all be authorised to manage the appraisal process for the Chair. It should take into account the views of trustees and, significantly, of the Chief Executive. Feedback should include suggestions for areas where the Chair can build skills.

Not all development opportunities need to be linked to appraisal. The Chief Executive can support the Chair by helping identify specific skill-building training that will help improve meetings and strengthen leadership. Professionally administered Chair inductions, specific skill training courses, networking and coaching opportunities can help the Chair develop the skills s/he needs to lead the board and support the Chief Executive.

Part 3

Crafting support for the Chair

Don't know what help to offer the Chair? Start by having conversations around specific areas of responsibility:

- meeting quality
- agenda setting
- facilitation and enabling techniques
- regulatory updates
- environmental awareness and analysing trends
- dealing with conflict
- managing committees
- building peer networks with other Chairs

Promoting board development

The Chair and the Chief Executive both have an interest in improving governance practice on the trustee board. The Chair's leadership role in this area is obvious: as head of the board, s/he needs to look for ways of constantly improving board effectiveness. Yet the Chief Executive too can be highly influential in getting the board to seek development. In fact, NCVO's research indicates that the idea of getting training and development for the board frequently originates with the Chief Executive.

For many Chief Executives and Chairs, the trickiest part of seeking development is first introducing the idea to the organisation. Many trustees have never heard of it and may be sceptical. Some may see it as a waste of precious organisational resources. In this case the Chair and Chief Executive can work together to introduce the idea gradually, providing information and examples. Use publications from organisations like NCVO and the Governance Hub to raise awareness of governance and practice issues. Review governance websites, subscribe to a sector magazines. See the Resources section for suggestions.

Board groups more attuned to the idea of development can begin to set targets for themselves, building development activities into their annual schedule. They may want to undertake a skills assessment or a governance review to pinpoint areas that need work. Or they may wish to schedule an away day or retreat to discuss governance issues. Some groups may decide to hire consultants to help them carry out this work, or they can choose one of a number of self-assessment tools available from NCVO and other organisations.

Sometimes the best way to lead is by example. Chief Executives and Chairs can help promote the idea of development by participating together in training that is appropriate for both parties. While roles differ, principles remain the same, so general courses in roles, current issues in regulation and governance can give Chief Executives and Chairs the opportunity to learn together. Together, they can bring back their new insights to the organisation and begin to implement changes.

Bad times for building partnerships

In certain circumstances, even the most committed Chief Executives and Chairs may find it difficult to make their partnership work. If your organisation is facing the following situations, your Chief Executive and Chair may find it impossible to make the most of their joint leadership role.

When the relationship is structurally flawed

Don't expect the Chair/Chief Executive partnership to function optimally if your organisation has set it up incorrectly in the first place. It may work, but it won't work as well as it should. Double check the governing document and the current role descriptions for both the Chief Executive and Chair to make certain that your practices are in keeping with the current recommendations. Identify built-in tensions and areas where problems can be addressed. Acknowledge areas of ambiguity, paradigm shifts and paradoxes in the relationship.

When the relationship is new

When a new Chief Executive joins the organisation or a new Chair steps up, it takes time to establish a working relationship. It's reasonable to expect some rough patches in the early days. Adequate support for both parties (good induction practices, communication systems and individual support in the form of skill training, mentoring or coaching) helps new partners establish a modus operandi more quickly.

During periods of disruptive change

Big changes to the organisation can bring instability to all its relationships. If your organisation is facing a major shake-up, it may be wise to wait until things begin to return to normal before you attempt to change the way your Chief Executive and Chair work together.

When the organisation is in crisis

Improving Chief Executive/Chair working practices is a strategic act that takes time, planning, good will and determination. An organisation in crisis is in no condition to give it the kind of attention it needs. As a rule, it's better to handle the crisis first, then turn your attention to matters of policy and practice when things settle down.

When trust has been lost

Even good practice can't help a relationship where trust has been lost. Don't try to introduce new ways of doing things until you've addressed this key factor in partnership. Try to identify ways to re-establish trust. Build confidence by offering mediation or facilitated discussions, or consider a change of personnel.

Dealing with conflict

Whenever people work together, disagreements will arise. In fact, structured disagreement forms part of a healthy working relationship between the Chief Executive and Chair as these two independently minded individuals bring their own ideas and perspectives to the table. The problem develops when disagreement spills over into conflict. Because conflict between Chief Executive and Chair is so damaging to governance effectiveness, boards and individuals need to take steps to confront the issue head on.

Avoiding conflict

Clear governance systems, procedures and codes of conduct such as those recommended in this guide go a long way toward minimising the risk of Chief Executive/ Chair disagreement turning into conflict. They bring clarity to group and individual interaction and provide a point of reference when doubts arise. They encourage ownership of behavioural and procedural norms by all parties. By anticipating and addressing areas where there is a risk of conflict, they prevent the danger of disagreement turning into something more serious.

Additionally, in order to avoid Chief Executive/Chair conflict, organisations need to establish a system for dealing with complaints and grievances. Although most organisations have such a system for volunteers and members of staff, there is often no clear procedure for the Chair or the Chief Executive. The system should be confidential, fair and transparent, providing a safe place for both leaders to come and be heard. Those charged with hearing Chief Executive and Chair grievances, whether they are board members, staff or trusted outsiders, need to be fully briefed and have the authority to make recommendations to the trustee board for further action. Furthermore, they should be familiar with conflict resolution strategies such as facilitation and mediate, see below.

Preventing conflict

- Listen with your full attention
- Respect confidentiality
- Behave as you would want others to behave
- Do not take an aggressive attitude
- Review communication systems regularly
- Frequently review your priorities
- Be clear about your own responsibility but flexible in helping others
- Encourage others' ideas and give them constructive feedback
- Respect and nourish diversity
- Ask questions when the situation is unclear
- Identify the problem
- When discussing opposing views, look for common ground
- Avoid making judgements
- Avoid making assumptions
- Don't share details of the conflict with those not directly involved
- Identify and specify personal conflicts of interest
- When a dispute arises, deal with it: denial won't work
- Wherever humanly possible, separate the person from the problem

Linda Laurance,
Workshop, Barclays Leadership Programme, May 2006

Handling conflict when it arises

Some Chief Executive/Chair relationships are in deep trouble. The problems may arise from a clash of personalities, confusion about roles, or a fundamental disagreement about organisational strategy. Whatever its origin, prolonged conflict between top leaders can poison an organisation. It the most serious cases, Chief Executive/Chair disagreements are divisive, sap morale and endanger the organisation's reputation. Some disputes – too many – end up in court, with attendant high costs and bitter feelings on both sides.

The good practice recommendations in this guide are designed to prevent such disputes from erupting in the first place. But, when conflict does occur, organisations can help restore harmony by taking steps to seek solutions. When Chief Executives and Chairs are locked in disagreement, others in the organisation may be drawn in, too, or they may simply lack the skills to sort things out. In this case, trained outsiders can help, bringing objectivity and specialist skills to the table.

Facilitated discussion

Facilitation by a third party can help troubled partnerships move on by enabling Chief Executives and Chairs to have the discussions they need to have without making the situation worse. In some circumstances, a trusted board member or staff member can take on the role of facilitator, provided s/he has the skills and experience to do the job. Many organisations find that hiring a facilitator from outside brings a high level of skill, objectivity and confidentiality to the negotiation process.

Mediation

Mediation is a process in which a professional mediator, or mediators, work with the individuals involved in the dispute to reach a resolution both parties can accept. It is an intensive process, calling for the cooperation of everyone involved in the conflict. Be aware that mediation is not a cheap or easy option: it can be both time consuming and expensive. Nonetheless, it is usually much cheaper than going to court and it is a powerful tool for overcoming the corrosive effects of conflict on the Chief Executive /Chair partnership. Once those locked in conflict can move forward, so can the organisation. For more information about where to find mediation services, see Resources.

Affordable professional mediation

The NCVO/CEDR subsidised scheme offers an affordable five-hour mediation session to voluntary and community sector organisations. Fees are fixed and depend on the size of the organisation and the nature of the dispute (for example, whether it is internal or external). CEDR Solve can appoint a mediator or provide a small panel from which the organisation can select a mediator of their choice. They can also provide neutral facilitators, Chairs and other kinds of consultants. See the Resources for information on how to contact CEDR Solve and learn more.

Chief Executives and Chairs in trouble

You know you need help when...

- you don't want to take your opposite number's call
- you dread board meetings
- you feel isolated and have no-one to confide in
- you fear your appraisal will be negative even though you're trying your best
- you're hiding the reality of the situation from your opposite number
- you feel you cannot admit you're in trouble or ask for help
- you believe that even if you asked for help you wouldn't get it
- you are afraid to go away on holiday

Part 4

Resources

Organisations

ACEVO

The professional body for third sector Chief Executives, ACEVO offers publications, events and training for executives.

Tel: 0845 345 8481
Web: www.acevo.org.uk

CEDR Solve

CEDR Solve is a consultancy offering a range of mediation and conflict resolution services. Call or visit their website for more information.

Tel: 020 7536 6060
Web: mediate@cedr-solve.com

Charity Commission

Publications, advice and all the latest in regulation.

Tel: 0845 300 0218
Web: www.charity-commission.gov.uk

Governance Hub

A government funded initiative that offers useful information on many aspects of governance practice . Download or order a free copy of *Good Governance: a code for the voluntary and community sector.*

Tel: 020 7520 2514
Web: www. governancehub.org.uk

NCVO

NCVO offers publications, advice, training and events for third sector organisations plus the Barclay's Leadership Programme for Chief Executives and Chairs.

Tel: 020 7713 6161
Web: www.ncvo-vol.org.uk

Publications

'You're not listening to me!' Dealing with disputes: mediation and its benefits for voluntary organisations, Linda Laurance and Anne Radford, NCVO Publications

A Polished Performance: findings from NCVO's leadership programme for Chief Executives and Chairs by Tesse Akpeki, NCVO publications

Best Behaviour: using trustee codes of conduct to improve governance practice by Tesse Akpeki, NCVO Publications

The Chair's First 100 days: a practical guide to the basics of board leadership by Tesse Akpeki, NCVO Publications

The Board Answer Book edited by Tesse Akpeki, NCVO Publications

Better Communication = Better Governance? by Tesse Akpeki and Tess Woodcraft, NCVO Publications

Setting Chief Executive Officer remuneration by Tesse Akpeki, NCVO Publications

Recruiting a New Chief Executive: a guide for trustees and Chairs by Dorothy Dalton, NCVO Publications

Good governance: the Chair's role by Dorothy Dalton, NCVO Publications

Leading the organisation: the relationship between Chairs and Chief Executives, ACEVO Publications

Partners in leadership: a new style of governance and management for charities, ACEVO Publications

Appraising the Chief Executive: a guide to performance review, ACEVO Publications

It's tough at the top: the no-fibbing guide to leadership by Debra Allock Tyler, DSC Publications

Daring to lead 2006 (A National study of NonProfit Leadership) by CompassPoint NonProfit Services and Meyer Foundation

Governance as leadership: reframing the work of nonprofit boards bt Richard Chait, William Ryan & Barbara Taylor, BoardSpace

Tiny essentials of an effective volunteer board by Ken Burnett , The White Lion Press Ltd

Resources

Model documents for the role of Chair

The following Chair job description and person specification are designed to give organisations a clearer idea of what these important documents should look like. They are only templates: to serve to your organisation, your board must adapt them through a process of discussion and decision-making. The serving Chair can provide insights into the reality of the role. Both job description and person specification should be reviewed and revised periodically to keep up with changing organisational needs.

Chair job description

Responsibilities as a trustee

- The Chair will continue to fulfil all those duties and responsibilities he/she assumed when he/she became a trustee.
- The Chair will abide by the Trustee Code of Conduct.
- The Chair will act in accordance with any additional organisational policies relating to trustee activity.

General Chair responsibilities

Providing leadership for the board as it fulfils its governance duties and responsibilities toward the organisation including:

- setting vision, values, mission, strategy and high-level policy in accordance with charity regulations and the governing document;
- monitoring the organisation's performance against established targets;
- securing financial stability for the organisation;
- protecting and managing organisational property and investments;
- safeguarding the organisation's reputation and values;
- making sure all organisational activities comply with regulations and the law;
- reviewing major risks and making provisions for the organisation to respond appropriately;
- appointing and managing the Chief Executive Officer (Chief Executive);
- organising and leading board development activities such as self-assessments;
- delegating the above duties appropriately.

Specific duties

Meetings

- **Planning meeting schedules and setting agendas:** The Chair establishes dates, times and locations of meetings and sets meeting agendas according to board procedures.
- **Leading meetings:** The Chair leads meetings and facilitates discussion, encouraging all trustees to participate and preventing more talkative members from dominating the debate.
- **Keeping trustees informed:** The Chair establishes and monitors systems for distributing information before meetings and keeping trustees updated between meetings.
- **Acting as a point of contact between meetings:** The Chair makes him/herself available to trustees and others for contact between meetings.

Board leadership

- **Building the board:** The Chair leads trustee recruitment and induction, strengthening the group by finding capable new trustees and providing for Chair succession.
- **Engaging the whole board:** The Chair uses the skills and interests of all board members and does not allow cliques or inner circles to form.
- **Developing governance effectiveness:** The Chair improves overall board effectiveness by taking steps to increase governance ability in the group and in individual trustees.
- **Seeking self-development:** The Chair seeks to improve governance practice by continually seeking to improve his or her own performance. S/he encourages feedback and responds appropriately.
- **Overseeing the work of committees:** The Chair oversees the establishment and activities of board committees, ensuring that they are accountable and report properly to the board.
- **Dealing with conflict on the board:** The Chair monitors and addresses conflict among board members and between trustees and other parts of the organisation.

Policy

- **Giving direction to board policy-making:** The Chair exercises leadership by setting priorities for the board and steering discussion toward strategic issues.
- **Monitoring the implementation of board decisions:** The Chair ensures that board decisions are communicated and implemented properly.

Representing the organisation

- **Acting as a spokesperson for the organisation:** The Chair speaks for the organisation when authorised.
- **Representing the organisation:** The Chair represents the organisation at public gatherings when asked.

Where staff are employed

- **Coordinating board management of the Chief Executive:** The Chair leads the board as it fulfils its management responsibilities toward the Chief Executive, overseeing role definition, selection, contracting, training, assessment and discipline.
- **Working with the Chief Executive Officer:** The Chair works with the Chief Executive on behalf of the board, coordinating efforts between the governing body and the executive. The Chair meets regularly with the Chief Executive to discuss strategic issues. S/he leads Chief Executive assessment, provides feedback, supports the Chief Executive and offers him/her appropriate development opportunities.
- **Developing the board with the Chief Executive:** Together the Chief Executive and Chair seek ways to improve board effectiveness by identifying development opportunities for the board and for the Chair.
- **Addressing conflict in the organisation:** The Chair monitors conflict in the organisation. He or she is available to help the Chief Executive, staff, trustees and others resolve conflicts. He or she takes steps to address conflict, acting to protect the organisation's reputation and preserve morale.
- **Sitting on appointment and disciplinary panels:** The Chair represents the board on appointment and disciplinary panels, especially those for the Chief Executive Officer.

Chair person specification

Essentials

- Commitment to the organisation
- Understanding of the legal duties, responsibilities and liabilities of trusteeship
- Willingness to put time and effort into the Chair role
- Respected and trusted by other board members

Personal qualities

- Good, independent judgement
- Impartiality, fairness and confidentiality
- Willingness to speak his or her mind
- Tact and diplomacy
- Respect for others
- Willingness to learn new skills

Specific abilities

- Strategic vision
- Creative thinking
- Leading meetings
- Working effectively as a team member
- Good communication and interpersonal skills

Experience

- Previous chairing experience (preferred but not required)
- Previous leadership position
- Experience of committee work

Model documents for the role of Chief Executive

The following Chief Executive job description and person specification are designed to give organisations a clearer idea of what these important documents should look like. They are only templates: to serve to your organisation, the trustee board needs to adapt them through a process of discussion and decision-making. The serving Chief Executive can provide insights into the reality of the role. Both job description and person specification should be reviewed and revised periodically to keep up with changing organisational needs.

Chief Executive job description

General responsibilities

Providing leadership to the organisation and to take responsibility for its management and administration within the strategic and accountability frameworks established by the board of trustees.

With the Chair, enabling the board of trustees to fulfil its duties and responsibilities for the proper governance of the organisation and to see to it that the board receives advice and information in a timely, thorough and appropriate manner.

Specific Duties

Working with the board

- With the Chair, seeing to it that the board of trustees formulates and regularly reviews the organisation's vision, mission and values;
- In partnership with trustees, developing a long-term strategy for the organisation within the vision, mission and values established by the board;
- With the Chair, ensuring that the board can adequately monitor annual plans, targets and performance;
- Reporting to the board on organisational progress, providing information and answering for organisational performance;
- With the Chair, developing policy proposals for board discussion and decision;
- With the Chair, establishing the annual calendar for board and subcommittee meetings;
- Supporting the Chair, suggesting development opportunities as appropriate;
- Enabling the board to broaden its capabilities and develop its leadership potential.

Leading and managing the organisation

- Ensuring that a long-term strategy is in place to guide the organisation in achieving its objectives;
- Being responsible to trustees for the overall financial health of the organisation;
- Ensuring that the organisation has the human, material and financial resources it needs to operate effectively;
- Seeking out and developing new strategies for ensuring future resources;
- Taking appropriate steps to protect the organisation from risk;
- Seeing to it that the organisation fulfils its constitutional, regulatory and legal obligations;
- Ensuring that the organisation has the right management systems and structures to carry out its work effectively, accountably and safely;
- Providing leadership to the management team and direction to all staff;
- Ensuring that staff, volunteers and others working in the organisation are focussed on achieving the mission and strategic priorities.

Promoting the organisation

- Protecting and enhancing the reputation of the organisation;
- Seeking opportunities to expand and promote awareness of the organisation's work;
- Using the media appropriately to raise the organisation's profile:
- Acting as spokesperson when authorised;

- Assisting in the formulation of marketing strategies and campaigns;
- Ensuring that marketing materials and other communications accurately and persuasively present the vision, mission and values of the organisation;
- Cooperating with fundraising staff, advising on grants, taking part in campaigns and meeting funders when necessary;
- Overseeing the regular updating of the website, production of the newsletter and other communications with supporters.

Chief Executive person specification

Essentials

- Commitment to the organisation's vision, values and mission
- Personal integrity and credibility
- Commitment to self-development
- Dedication to developing the organisation

Personal qualities

- Charisma
- Tact
- Responsiveness
- Realism
- Honesty
- Enthusiasm

Specific abilities

- Financial and management expertise
- Content and programme expertise
- Excellent communication and people skills
- Ability to build networks and make connections
- Strategic orientation
- Ability to take the lead
- Team player

Experience

- Track record of general management at the senior executive level
- Proven ability to work successfully with a trustee board
- Experience in managing an organisation of comparable size
- Knowledge of voluntary and community sector governance practice